THE CODE
OF LIFE

Alvin Silverstein

and

Virginia Silverstein

Illustrated by
Kenneth Gosner

DOVER PUBLICATIONS, INC.
Mineola, New York

For Bella and Benjamin Mayer

Bibliographical Note

This Dover edition, first published in 2004, is an unabridged republication
of the work originally published by Atheneum, New York, in 1972. A new pref-
ace has been specially prepared by the authors for the present edition.

Library of Congress Cataloging-in-Publication Data

Silverstein, Alvin.
    The code of life / Alvin Silverstein and Virginia Silverstein ; illustrated by
Kenneth Gosner.
        p. cm.
    "This Dover edition, first published in 2004, is an unabridged republica-
tion of the work originally published by Atheneum, New York, in 1972"—
T.p. verso.
    Includes index.
    ISBN 0-486-43944-5 (pbk.)
    1. Genetic code—Juvenile literature. I. Silverstein, Virginia B. II. Gosner,
Kenneth L., 1925– III. Title.

QH450.2.S54 2004
572.8'633—dc22

2004049365

Manufactured in the United States of America
Dover Publications, Inc., 31 East 2nd Street, Mineola, N.Y. 11501

Preface to the Dover Edition

Although *The Code of Life* was written more than thirty years ago, the concepts and achievements it describes have not become "dated." Rather, they have been confirmed and expanded by new studies, forming the foundation upon which a generation of researchers have been building. A knowledge of these concepts is essential to understanding the headline-making breakthroughs in genetics today.

The second half of the twentieth century was an exciting time: Scientists had learned that the "instruction manual" for every living thing is spelled out in a code of just four "letters" using various combinations of chemicals called DNA and RNA; researchers had figured out how these chemicals produce proteins that build and shape our bodies, as well as those of other animals and plants. The "code of life" spelled out in DNA and RNA is also translated into the proteins that run the chemical reactions that allow us to think, breathe, move, and eat. Researchers discovered the basic form of *chromosomes*—tiny structures inside each living cell that contain genes, the units of heredity—and learned how the DNA in these genes is copied and passed on from one generation to another. They learned to "read" gene structure and to build copies of genes, even changing their structure to correct nature's errors or to work out new designs. It was the beginning of a scientific adventure filled with great promise.

As years went by, determinations of gene sequences—the order of the letters, or "bases," spelling out DNA with instructions for making a particular protein—went from a rare event reported in the news media to an everyday routine. *Sequenators,* automated machines that can be programmed to run the series of chemical reactions needed to determine a DNA sequence, were built. Automatic gene synthesizers became standard equipment in a modern molecular genetics lab, where genes could be made to order. Researchers were gradually mapping the chromosomes of humans and other organisms and learning where particular genes were located. So much progress was made, so quickly, that in 1990 the Human Genome Project was launched. This major international effort, funded by the U.S. government and private companies, had an ambitious goal: to map and sequence all of the DNA in human chromosomes. This huge task was scheduled for completion by 2005, but was finished ahead of time. In June 2000, two separate research teams announced that they had completed a first draft of the entire sequence of the human genome. Dozens of other genomes have since been sequenced, including those of chimpanzees, dogs, mice, fruit flies, yeast, worms, plants, and bacteria.

A genome sequence gives the order of the chemical "letters" spelling out the hereditary instructions but does not tell what particular genes do, or how they work. However, a careful analysis of various parts of the sequence, comparing them with similar parts of the chromosomes of other species or with genes whose functions are already known, can yield much information. This is an enormous task: a single gene contains thousands of "letters," and the DNA in just one chromosome can contain millions of them. Determining gene sequences, mapping the individual genes, and analyzing their roles would have been impossible without the fantastic development of computers over the past few decades. Today's computers not only can perform huge numbers of mathematical calculations far faster than a human brain can, but they can also search for and recognize patterns within a great mass of information—a task that an unaided brain would find hopelessly confusing. Today's genetics research teams typically include computer specialists, who write programs to help make sense out of the flood of new information.

Long before the first genome was sequenced, the growing knowledge of and insight into genes and their workings began to find important applications: in the early 1980s, for example, when the AIDS epidemic first appeared, researchers had the tools to find out a great deal about this new and deadly virus. In an amazingly short time they were able to work out the chemical structure of all of the genes in the AIDS virus and determine how each one helps the virus invade human cells, survive, and spread. This knowledge has helped devise drugs targeted specifically against particular parts of the virus's life cycle. Similar approaches are being used in the fight against other diseases.

Fundamental knowledge of the code of life also provides insights into genetic diseases caused by changes in genes that make some body organs or systems unable to work properly. Scientists have discovered that *oncogenes* (tumor-causing genes) can lead to cancer; other genes normally present in our cells help prevent cancer from developing. The role of genes in other common diseases such as heart disease and diabetes is also being explored. Medical researchers are attempting to develop cures for a number of diseases, from cancer to sickle-cell anemia and cystic fibrosis, using gene therapy (the modification of genes to correct or compensate for harmful mutations).

Genetic engineering is being used to produce animals and plants that provide more nutritious foods, such as fruits and vegetables resistant to molds and diseases, protein-enriched grains, and meats with modified fats that protect against heart disease rather than promoting it. Transgenic plants and animals, whose genomes include genes from other species, are being used as living factories—"pharms"—to mass-produce drugs and other useful products. Genetic knowledge is revolutionizing crime detection, as well. A single hair, a drop of blood, or the saliva residues left after licking the glue on an envelope can yield DNA that may identify a criminal—or free an innocent person. Each person's DNA provides a unique "fingerprint" in a pattern like a bar code, which can be compared with samples from a crime scene. DNA fingerprints can also help trace family relationships and are useful in mapping the migrations of ancient peoples and the evolution of humans and other species.

Basic research into the code of life has not ended with the mapping of the human genome but is continuing enthusiastically. Scientists are encountering new mysteries: for example, in most organisms, genes are not neatly strung along the chromosome like beads. The portions of DNA in a chromosome that contain the code to make a protein are typically interspersed among stretches of DNA that do not seem to "spell out" any meaningful message. In fact, the coding sequence of a gene is usually interrupted by long stretches of bases that seem to be merely taking up space. These interruptions, or *introns,* are removed during the process of protein-making, much the way you might edit out the commercials interrupting a TV show if you were recording it. Scientists at first thought that this extra DNA was "junk," produced accidentally and preserved when the DNA in the chromosomes was copied during cell division. Now they suspect that the "junk" DNA may have some value, such as providing "on–off" switches and other controls to regulate the work of the genes, or performing as raw materials for new genes. And it seems that much of this "junk" may contain instructions for making pieces of RNA that act as *enzymes* (chemicals that help other chemicals to react), regulators of genes or proteins, or play various other roles in the cells. Researchers have found in plants and animals hundreds of types of small RNA molecules that help to determine what proteins are produced in a cell, when they are produced, and in what amounts. Small "interfering" RNAs are being used to fight disease-causing viruses and to regulate various cell functions. As both knowledge and applications expand, this new area of genetic research seems to be at a stage reminiscent of DNA research in the early 1970s—an era filled with both puzzles and promise.

We hope you'll enjoy revisiting that time of discovery, and better understand and appreciate the amazing world of today.

Alvin and Virginia Silverstein, April 2004

Contents

THE CODE
OF LIFE

The Patterns of Life

WHY DOES A CAT HAVE KITTENS AND NOT PUPPIES? WHY do a hen's eggs hatch into chicks instead of ducklings? Why does an acorn grow into an oak tree instead of a sunflower? Everywhere, Nature seems to have things in order.

Even people follow Nature's rules. Not only do humans have human babies, but, when they grow up, the children often look very much like their parents. Why should this be so?

For many years, man did not know the answers to these questions. Even now we do not know all the answers. But scientists have learned much, and each day they are learning more and more.

A cat and a chicken, a tree and a man surely seem very different. A cat has fur and claws; a chicken has feathers and a beak. A tree has a trunk and leaves, and a man has a mind that can think and plan and hands that can shape things to make his plans come true.

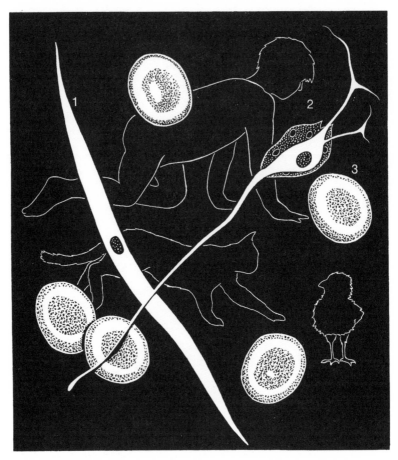

Smooth muscle cells (1), nerve cells (2), and red blood cells (3).

But cats and chickens, trees and men, and all the other living things in our world are very much alike in many ways. They are made up of countless numbers of tiny building blocks called cells. These cells are so small that they cannot be seen without a microscope. The cells of a living creature are specialists, each with its own set of jobs that help to keep the whole organism alive and well. They are shaped in various ways according to the jobs they do. Yet under a microscope, the cells of a cat, a chick, a tree, and even a man are surprisingly alike.

Each cell has a *nucleus*, a tiny mass containing important chemicals of life. The nucleus is like a master control center for the cell. It contains the plans for the chemicals that are made in the cell and helps to direct the thousands of chemical reactions that go on inside the cell. Chemical messengers constantly pass in and out of the nucleus. Some bring in information about what is going on in the cell and what new chemicals are needed. Others carry out sets of blueprints that will be used for building new materials. For the cell must not only do its own jobs in the body, but must also repair itself if anything goes wrong, and it may even make more cells like itself. The information needed to direct all these activities is found inside the nucleus.

The nucleus is enclosed in a thin covering called a *membrane* that is something like a tiny plastic bag. But this is a rather leaky bag, more like a sieve. For there are tiny holes in the membrane through which many small chemicals can freely pass back and forth. And large chemicals, even the most complicated chemicals of life, can be sent through the nuclear membrane, too.

The cell itself is also surrounded by a membrane, the *cell membrane*. Food materials, oxygen, and various chemical messengers come to the cell from other parts of the body and enter it through the cell membrane. The cell's waste products and chemical messengers of its own pass out through the membrane and are carried to other parts of the body.

The material of the cell, outside the nucleus, is called the *cytoplasm*. It was once thought that the cytoplasm was a watery fluid, held together by the cell membrane. It was also thought that various chemicals floated about

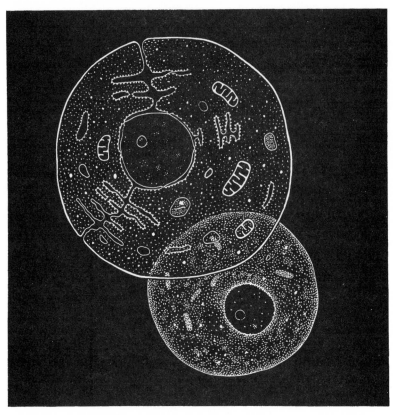

A cell, as seen through an electron microscope (top) and a light microscope (bottom).

in the cytoplasm, so that the cell was something like a plastic bag filled with alphabet soup.

This was the way the cell appeared to be under the best light microscopes. But then the electron microscope was developed, and scientists were able to see much smaller things. They were able to look at the thin cell membrane and at structures inside the cell. They soon discovered that the cell is far more complicated and better organized than they had thought.

Running from the cell membrane in to the nuclear membrane is a branching, crisscrossing network of membranes that divide the cytoplasm into many tiny compartments. This network of membranes is called the *endoplasmic reticulum* (reticulum comes from a word meaning "net") or *ER*. The ER is like a network of highways, along which chemicals are sent through the cell. Many important reactions take place at busy intersections of the ER.

An amazing number of chemical reactions go on constantly in the living cell. Chemicals are built up and broken down. Oxygen is added to other chemicals in reactions that supply energy for the cell's activities.

Each cell of the body contains thousands and thousands of different kinds of chemicals. The structures of the cell are built from very large chemical compounds, whose units, or molecules, each may contain hundreds, thousands, or even millions of atoms. Proteins are among the most important structural substances of the cell. Fatty substances are built into some of the cell proteins. Other cell structures are formed from *polysaccharides*, chemicals built up from many small sugar units, linked together. Dissolved in the liquids of the cell and attached to its structures are sugars, salts, and even gases such as oxygen and carbon dioxide. These chemicals are small compounds, whose molecules may contain only a few atoms.

All the chemical reactions that take place in the cell are controlled by a special type of protein, called *enzymes*. Enzymes have very large molecules, twisted and folded into a fantastic variety of shapes. Some of the bumps and hollows on the outside of an enzyme molecule are just the right size and shape for other, smaller molecules to fit onto them. And they have just the right atoms, arranged in just the right way, to hold onto these

7

smaller molecules by chemical forces. Some enzymes bring two different small molecules together and help them to join into a new, larger molecule. Other enzymes help to break larger molecules apart or change them in some other way. Enzymes determine how fast chemical reactions take place. The enzymes themselves are not changed in these reactions. A single enzyme molecule can be used over and over again.

The set of chemicals in a cell from the toe is mostly the same as that in a cell from the heart or the brain. But some cells may have more of one chemical than another and may even have a few special enzymes and other chemicals to help them do their own jobs.

Scientists who study the chemicals of the living cell—how they are made and how their reactions help cells to do their jobs—are called molecular biologists. They study the molecules of life.

The cells of the body work together, each doing its own special job that helps to keep the whole organism healthy and strong. And though these cells are built from the same kinds of chemicals and all have the same important parts—a nucleus and cytoplasm and membranes—they are shaped differently, according to the jobs they do. Nerve cells, which carry messages through the body, are like long threads with a knot near one end. Some of the cells of the skin look like pavement stones and help to keep germs outside the body. If germs do sneak in, they may be gobbled up by white blood cells. These "policemen" of the body are like blobs of jelly and can change their shape with ease.

Special cells, called sex cells, can start off a new life. Men have tiny sperm cells that look like wiggly tadpoles. Women have larger, round, egg cells that are filled with food materials. When an egg cell and a sperm cell join together, they grow into a baby.

A sperm cell from your father and an egg cell from your mother joined to make a new cell, which was the beginning of you. That is why you may look a little like your father and a little like your mother.

But how could two microscopic cells that look like a tiny tadpole and a round ball possibly form something as complicated as a human being? The answer lies inside the nucleus of each of these sex cells.

The Code of Life

IN THE NUCLEUS OF EACH CELL OF THE BODY IS A MASTER plan. This plan contains the blueprints for all the parts of the cells, the shapes and sizes of the cells of the body, and the jobs they do. There are plans for keeping the cells in good working order and for making new cells if parts of the body are damaged and need repair. There are even instructions for how tall a person can grow to be, how many fingers he has on each hand, the shape of his face, the color of his hair and eyes, and just about everything about him.

Each cell of the body has the same complete set of plans for the whole body. It seems strange that a cell in the tip of a toe should have the blueprints for making an eye and an ear, a heart, and all the other parts of the body. And even more amazing, each cell somehow seems to know exactly which blueprints to use and what parts to make.

How can a master plan with so many different blueprints all fit inside the tiny nucleus within each microscopic cell? These blueprints are neatly stored in special structures inside the nucleus, called *chromosomes.* Under a powerful microscope, the chromosomes look like tiny strings of beads.

The nucleus of a cell from a mosquito contains six chromosomes. The cells of a pea plant have 14. So do those of a cucumber. A cell from a cat has 38 chromosomes, while cells from a dog have 78. The cells of some butterflies have 380 tiny chromosomes.

Notice that these sets of chromosomes are all even numbers. Scientists have taken pictures of the chromosomes of cells through a microscope. In the pictures the chromosomes look like a confused jumble of rods of different sizes and shapes. Some are short and fat; others are long and thin. They may be curved, or bent into a shape like an L or a J or a V. If the chromosomes are carefully cut out of the picture, one at a time, the tiny scraps can be sorted according to size and shape. Then it is found that there are actually pairs of chromosomes —nearly every one has a "twin" that looks almost exactly like it. The human set of 46 chromosomes is made up of 23 different pairs. The cells of a pea plant each contain seven pairs of chromosomes. The cells of a tiny fruit fly contain four pairs of chromosomes.

Each human body cell has 46 chromosomes. But the sperm and the egg have only half as many, just 23 chromosomes each. And none of these are matching pairs— all 23 are different.

When a sperm and an egg join together to form a new cell which will grow into a baby, that first cell has 46 chromosomes, 23 from the father and 23 from the

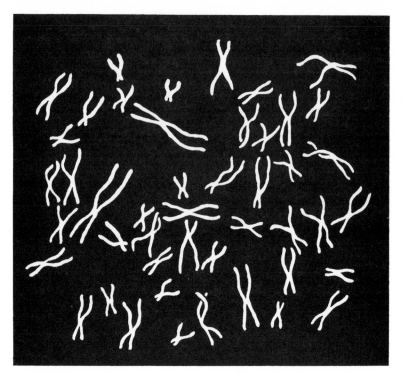

Human chromosomes.

mother. So you have only half of the plans from your father and half of the plans from your mother. That is why you may not look exactly like your father or exactly like your mother.

How can so much information be stored in such tiny structures as the chromosomes? The master plan is written out in a chemical language, spelled out in an amazing chemical called *DNA*.

DNA's official chemical name is *deoxyribonucleic acid*. This name comes from the name of a sugar (deoxyribose), which is part of DNA, and from the fact that it is a substance found in the nucleus of the cell. The molecules of DNA are the largest of all the chemicals of life—even larger than protein molecules. They may contain millions or even billions of atoms.

Scientists are still not sure how many DNA molecules are contained in each chromosome. There is probably just one DNA molecule in each chromosome of tiny viruses and bacteria. The chromosomes of animals and plants are larger and more complicated and probably each contain more than one DNA molecule. The chromosomes of these larger creatures also contain proteins, combined with the DNA. We do not yet know all about what the proteins in chromosomes do, although scientists are studying them and finding out more all the time. But science has found out an enormous amount about what DNA is and how it works.

For a long time DNA was quite a mystery. Scientists knew that the nucleus controls nearly all the activities of the cell, and almost all of the DNA in the cell is found in the nucleus. (Only small amounts are ever found anywhere else in a living cell.) It seemed that DNA must have something to do with the master plan. Yet it did not seem to be a complicated enough chemical to hold all that information.

Scientists had taken samples of DNA and broken them apart chemically, to see what they were made of. In the "chemical soup" that they obtained, they found the sugar deoxyribose and another chemical called phosphate. They also found various amounts of four different chemicals, all belonging to the same family, called organic bases. The bases that are found in DNA are called *adenine, thymine, guanine,* and *cytosine.* (Scientists usually abbreviate them as A, T, G, and C.) The amounts of the different bases vary according to the kind of creature from whose cells the DNA was taken. But amazingly, the cells of a tree and a cat, a chicken and a man, and even a microscopic germ, all have DNA with the same four bases, A, T, G, and C.

It did not seem logical that a chemical compound containing only four bases, a sugar, and phosphate could hold all the information needed to direct the activities of a living cell. Most scientists believed that the code of life must lie in a different kind of chemical, the proteins. Proteins are made up of varied combinations of twenty different building blocks, called *amino acids*. Twenty "letters" makes a quite respectable alphabet, and it was easy to see how information could be stored in proteins.

Yet what was all that DNA doing in the nucleus?

The big breakthrough came in 1953, in Cambridge, England. An English biochemist, Francis Crick, and a young American biochemist, James Watson, were working together on the DNA problem. They had gathered together the reports of many experiments giving bits of information about how parts of the DNA molecule were arranged. In 1953 they announced to the world that they had worked out a model of how the whole DNA molecule is put together.

Crick and Watson said that DNA is built like a double helix, which looks like a spiral staircase, winding round and round. The edges of the staircase are made up of bits of the sugar deoxyribose, joined together by phosphate groups. The steps of the staircase are made up of pairs of the four organic bases. The bases are paired up in quite definite ways. Adenine on one strand of the helix is always paired with thymine on the other, and guanine is always paired with cytosine. Thus, the "steps" .

DNA double helix: sugar deoxyribose at the edges joined together by small phosphate groups. "Stair steps" are the four organic bases, paired.

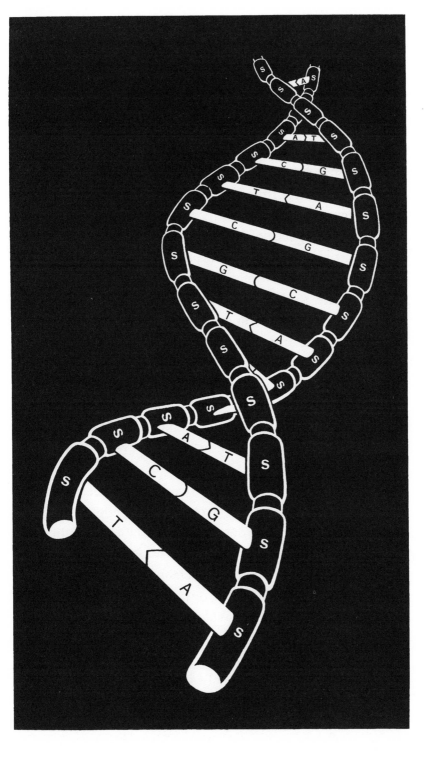

on the spiral staircase are always either AT or TA, GC or CG, and never any other combination.

Why should this be so? Why cannot two adenines join together, or an adenine and a cytosine? The strict "base pairing" rules that the bases of DNA follow are chemical rules. The bases are joined together by a special kind of chemical bond called a hydrogen bond. For two chemicals to form a hydrogen bond, one must have a hydrogen atom, and the other must have an atom of nitrogen or oxygen of a special kind. And all these atoms must be in just the right position to join together. Cytosine and guanine are held together in DNA by three separate hydrogen bonds. Adenine and thymine form only two. If adenine and cytosine were next to each other, their atoms would not be in the right places to form hydrogen bonds. And so this pair of bases could not hold the two chains of DNA together.

The double helix model proposed by Watson and Crick checked so well with everything that was known about the DNA molecule—how its parts are shaped and how they behave chemically—that the scientists of the world accepted it, even though the DNA molecule was too small to be seen in the electron microscopes of the time. It was not until 1969 that the double helix of a DNA molecule was seen for the first time in a photograph taken by a powerful electron microscope.

The Watson–Crick model did much more than just show how the DNA molecule is put together. It also provided important clues to how it works. For in the excitement that followed the announcement in 1953, many biologists and chemists began to study DNA, and soon they discovered that it does indeed carry the code of life.

16

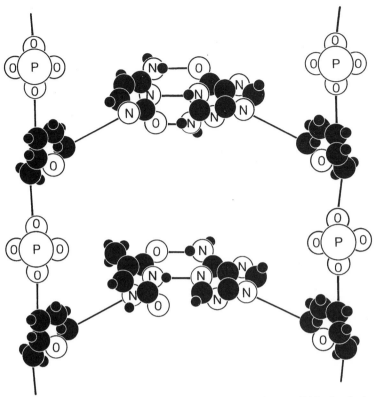

A molecular diagram, part of the DNA chain. The small black circles are hydrogen, the larger white circles, carbon. These show the composition of the sugar, phosphate, and bases.

How can all the information needed to make a chicken or a tree or a man be spelled out in an alphabet of just four letters? This is not really as impossible as it sounds. True, our alphabet has 26 letters. But any word or sentence in the English language can also be spelled out in Morse code, which is made up of only two "letters," dot and dash. Each individual word takes up more space than it does in our longer alphabet (... --- ... is much longer than SOS), but it can be spelled out.

Just how much space for messages is there in a DNA molecule? This chemical seems very small to us, so small that we cannot even see it. Yet, the DNA in each human chromosome has billions of bases.

If each of these bases was thought of as a letter, there would be more than a billion letters in the "words" spelled out in just one DNA molecule! If you started writing right now, and did not stop to eat or sleep, it would take you about thirty years to write a billion letters.

It is the order in which the "words" are spelled out with the four letter alphabet of heredity that determines whether a new baby is to be a dog, a cat, a gorilla, a whale, or a human. And it is the order of the letters that tells the body to make a hand with five fingers, or six, or four; or eyes that are blue or gray or green.

It is hard to imagine how many different orders of letters there could be on a whole DNA molecule. For the moment, we shall consider only the one chain of the double helix; if we know the order of the bases in that one, the base pairing rules will tell us what the order of the other chain must be. Suppose the single chain were only two bases long. Let us see how many different two-letter "words" could be spelled out with the four-letter alphabet of DNA bases. There are sixteen possibilities:

AA	AC	AG	AT
CA	CC	CG	CT
GA	GC	GG	GT
TA	TC	TG	TT

The number of possible words in the DNA "dictionary" goes up quickly when we add another base—another letter. Using the same four-letter alphabet, we can make 64 different words:

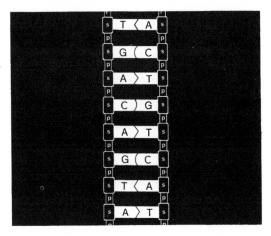

Another way to visualize the DNA chain, this is known as the "template scheme."

TTT	TAT	TTC	TAC	TTA	TAA	TTG	TAG
TCT	TGT	TCC	TGC	TCA	TGA	TCG	TGG
CTT	CAT	CTC	CAC	CTA	CAA	CTG	CAG
CCT	CGT	CCC	CGC	CCA	CGA	CCG	CGG
ATT	AAT	ATC	AAC	ATA	AAA	ATG	AAG
ACT	AGT	ACC	AGC	ACA	AGA	ACG	AGG
GTT	GAT	GTC	GAC	GTA	GAA	GTG	GAG
GCT	GGT	GCC	GGC	GCA	GGA	GCG	GGG

If we added another letter to the "word," we could have more than 250 different four letter "words." Imagine how much information can be packed into a whole DNA molecule! A single DNA molecule, with more than a billion letters, could spell out more different messages than there are grains of sand on all the world's beaches.

Just what is the code of life then? The DNA molecule is like a code book. Its messages are spelled out in a four-letter alphabet of bases. The bases are joined together in a very special order. They form words, which in turn are joined together to form sentences and paragraphs—the DNA molecules.

Eventually the DNA code must be translated into "words" spelled in a larger alphabet, the twenty-letter alphabet of protein molecules. Only then can the plans coded in DNA be put into action. DNA cannot do this by itself.

DNA carries the message of heredity in its code. And to put the code to work the DNA has special messengers, which carry its orders to the rest of the cell. These messengers are chemicals called *RNA*. It is through them that DNA directs the activities of the cell.

How DNA *Works*

THE NUCLEIC ACIDS ARE OFTEN CALLED THE "INFOR-mation molecules" of the cell. DNA stores the master plans for everything that goes on in a living organism. But without another kind of information molecule, RNA, these plans could never be carried out. There are several kinds of RNA, and they are all concerned with translating DNA's plans into action.

The formal name of RNA is *ribonucleic acid*. It contains a special sugar, ribose, which is chemically very much like deoxyribose, the sugar in DNA. Just as in DNA, molecules of sugar are linked together by phosphates to form the backbone of the RNA molecule.

Like DNA, RNA has four different kinds of organic bases. In fact, three of the bases are exactly the same as three of the DNA bases: A, C, and G. But T (thymine) is never found in RNA. Instead, it has a new base, *uracil* (which is abbreviated as U).

There is another big difference between RNA and

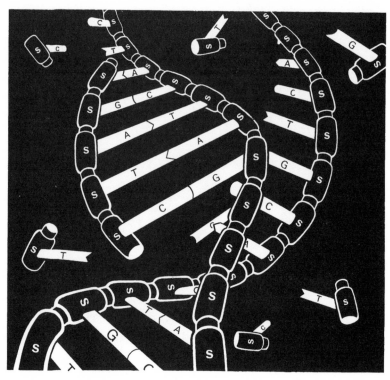

DNA splitting to begin forming RNA.

DNA. The spiral staircase of DNA is like a double chain. But RNA usually has just one chain, forming a single helix or spiral. The bases are not paired up, as they are in DNA.

Yet the bases of RNA can pair up, and sometimes they do. This is a very important part of how RNA is made and how it works.

DNA sends its orders to the cell by making RNA messengers. Each RNA molecule looks like part of the DNA molecule that made it.

When a DNA molecule is ready to make RNA, part of it unzips. The hydrogen bonds that hold the two chains together are not as strong as other kinds of chem-

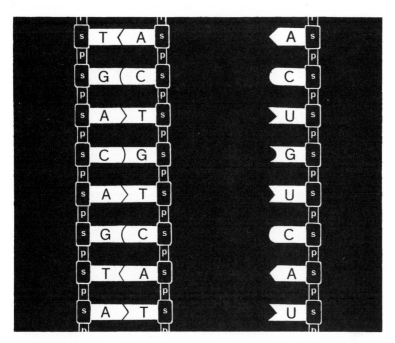

An RNA strand, to the right, made by the DNA double strand. The RNA was made by the left-hand DNA strand.

ical bonds. And so these bonds can break and the chains can separate without any damage to the chains themselves.

Special enzymes in the nucleus break the hydrogen bonds of part of the DNA, one by one, and the two chains of the helix start to unwind and come apart. Now the bases on the DNA chain become uncovered, each in its turn. Along one of the chains, an RNA base (attached to a sugar and phosphate), which was floating free in the nucleus, moves into place beside each DNA base that is uncovered. The RNA base must be just the right base, for the new molecule that is growing follows the same kind of pairing rules that governed the bases in the original double chain of DNA. The RNA base G will line up next to a C in the DNA, a C next to a G. An A will form a hydrogen bond with the T in DNA, and, since RNA never contains thymine, a U will be joined into place next to an A in DNA.

Soon a row of RNA bases, each attached to a sugar and a phosphate, forms next to the uncovered part of the DNA chain. The RNA bases are arranged in a very definite order. The RNA chain is not just like the DNA chain to which these bases are attached. Instead it is like making a model by pouring plaster into a mold. Wherever there will be a knob or ridge sticking out on the finished model, there will be a corresponding hollow or groove in the mold. In the same way, the order of bases in the RNA chain corresponds or is complementary to the DNA chain on which it is made. (In fact, except that RNA contains U instead of T, the order of bases in the new RNA chain is exactly the same as that in the other DNA chain, which was also complementary to the first.)

What happens to the other DNA chain? Why does it not form its own chain of RNA? That is one of the riddles that molecular biologists are still working on.

When the duplication process is over, a whole row of RNA bases has been formed, perhaps thousands of nucleotides long. (A *nucleotide* is a DNA or RNA base, attached to a sugar and a phosphate.) The RNA sugars and phophates link up together like a set of snap-together beads. After the RNA chain is made, it breaks away, and the two DNA chains coil up together again into a double helix. The new RNA molecule now has DNA's message, spelled out in thousands of bases. It is called messenger RNA.

Messenger RNA now goes out into the cytoplasm. Its job is to tell the cell how to make proteins. At tiny ball-like structures called *ribosomes*, the messenger RNA

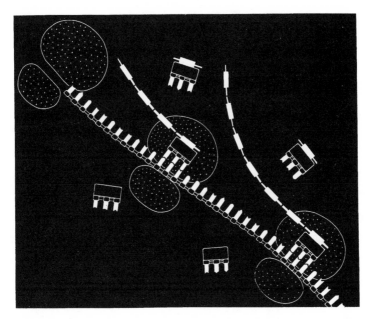

An RNA strand makes proteins of the ribosomes as transfer RNA brings in amino acids.

waits, while amino acids, the building blocks of the proteins, are brought to it.

There are about 20 different kinds of amino acids. When the right kinds in the right amounts are put together in the right way, they make a protein. Proteins are like long strings of beads of 20 different colors. Many patterns can be made using beads of these 20 colors, depending on how many of each are used and in what order they are strung. Nature has made millions of different proteins, each with its own pattern or sequence of amino acids. Each kind of animal and plant probably has some proteins that are found nowhere else in the living world. It is amazing what variety there can be with the same 20 basic building blocks. Hair and fingernails are made almost entirely of proteins. Our skin, our eyes—nearly every part of a human being—are built mainly of different kinds of proteins. Proteins help our blood to clot and carry signals that tell our bodies to grow. Some of the most important chemicals in the body are enzymes, proteins that help other chemicals to react.

The cell has a special "taxicab service" to bring the amino acids to the ribosomes to meet the messenger RNA with the plan for putting them together. There is a different kind of "taxicab" for each type of amino acid. The "taxicabs" are also RNA molecules—a different kind of RNA. They are called transfer RNA, because they transfer the amino acids to the ribosomes.

The transfer RNA molecules are much smaller than the messenger RNAs, and their job is much simpler. Messenger RNA carries the plans for a whole long protein molecule. But the transfer RNA just has to pick up its own special amino acid and line it up along the messenger RNA, to make a protein molecule.

Protein molecules are made at the ribosomes. These tiny structures have their own kind of RNA, called ribosomal RNA. This third type of RNA helps to "read out" the message by lining up the long messenger RNA molecules and matching them up with the right transfer RNA "taxicabs" carrying their amino acid "passengers."

As a protein starts to form, the end of a messenger RNA molecule becomes attached to a ribosome. A transfer RNA molecule with its amino acid is lined up next to it. Then the ribosome begins to move down the messenger RNA chain. Each time a space opens up, the right transfer RNA moves in to fill it. Soon there is a whole row of transfer RNA molecules lined up next to the messenger RNA. Each one is holding an amino acid. The amino acids link up together and form a chain of their own—a protein molecule. The sequence of amino acids in the new protein is determined by the sequence of bases in messenger RNA. And it is the sequence of amino acids in the protein that determines what kind of protein it will be.

The growing protein molecule looks like a dangling tail as the ribosome moves on. Finally the ribosome gets to the end of the messenger RNA molecule and drops off. The new protein molecule breaks away and goes off to do its jobs in the cell.

How are the amino acids lined up in just the right order? How is DNA's code translated from a four-letter alphabet of organic bases into a twenty-letter alphabet of amino acids? The answer lies in the RNA.

Nearly a decade after Watson and Crick worked out the model of how DNA is put together, scientists discovered that the code of life is spelled out in three-letter words, triplets of bases along the DNA chain. When DNA makes messenger RNA, the same code is spelled out in the RNA bases that line up along the DNA chain. For these RNA bases all had to line up in just the right way, according to the special pairing rules for bases. Each three-letter "word" in the messenger RNA molecule is called a *codon.*

The transfer RNA molecules also carry important messages. Each one may have 70 or 80 bases. Some parts of the molecule help it to pick up its own special amino acid and to make the amino acid ready to be built into a protein. One set of three bases in the transfer RNA molecule is special: it is part of the code of life. This triplet of bases is called an *anticodon.* Its

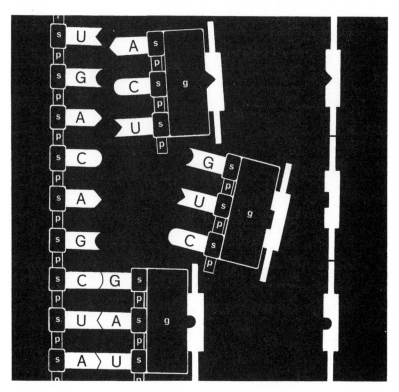

Protein synthesis, showing messenger and transfer RNA.

bases are in just the right order to pair up with a particular triplet or codon in the messenger RNA molecule.

For example, if the anticodon of a transfer RNA molecule contains the bases UCU, it will find a place on the messenger RNA that reads AGA. A different transfer RNA with an anticodon AAG will line up with a UUC codon of the messenger RNA. And so on for all the different three-letter codes. Each time the codon and anticodon will pair up according to the usual base-pairing rules.

So that is how the DNA code of life is translated into proteins. The DNA is used as a model or "template," which is faithfully copied in the form of messenger RNA. The messenger RNA molecule carries the triplet code out to the ribosomes. There it is matched up with a series of transfer RNA molecules, each of which contains the corresponding triplet anti-codons. Each of the lined-up transfer RNA molecules is carrying its own particular amino acid, and these are linked together into a protein. Thus, each three-letter codon corresponds to one "letter" or amino acid in the twenty-letter alphabet of proteins.

The genetic code was worked out through many painstaking experiments. Artificial RNA molecules were made in the laboratory, then mixed with transfer RNA's, amino acids, and enzymes to see what kind of proteins would be made. For example the transfer RNA polyuridylic acid (poly-U) is a chemical made of a long chain of uracil bases, each connected to a ribose sugar and phosphate. When poly-U is used as a template, a very strange "protein" is formed: poly-phenylalanine. This is a long chain containing many molecules of just one amino acid, phenylalanine. No matter how many other amino acids and transfer RNAs are present, only phenylalanine is built into the protein when poly-U is used as the pattern. This shows that the UUU codon corresponds to phenylala-nine, since that is the only codon that can exist in poly-U.

Another kind of experiment also helped to give in-formation about the genetic code. Working with viruses, the simplest forms of life, biochemists have been able to determine the structures of some of the proteins and parts of the nucleic acid that makes them. By matching up the proteins and the corresponding parts of the nucleic acids, they have been able to figure out parts of the code.

In these ways, a complete dictionary for translating the genetic code has now been drawn up. Each three-letter codon listed on the right is matched to the corresponding amino acid on the left. And that amino acid is built into a protein only when the messenger RNA contains one of the correct codons for that amino acid.

AMINO ACID	CODONS
Alanine	GCU, GCC, GCG, GCA
Arginine	AGG, AGA, CGU, CGC, CGG, CGA
Asparagine	AAU, AAC
Aspartic acid	GAU, GAC
Cysteine	UGU, UGC
Glutamic acid	GAG, GAA
Glutamine	CAG, CAA
Glycine	GGU, GGC, GGG, GGA
Histidine	CAU, CAC
Isoleucine	AUU, AUC, AUA
Leucine	UUG, UUA, CUU, CUG, CUC, CUA
Lysine	AAG, AAA
Methionine	AUG
Phenylalanine	UUU, UUC
Proline	CCU, CCC, CCG, CCA
Serine	UCU, UCC, UCG, UCA, AGU, AGC
Threonine	ACU, ACC, ACG, ACA
Tryptophan	UGG
Tyrosine	UAU, UAC
Valine	GUU, GUC, GUG, GUA
Start signals	AUG, GUG
Stop signals	UGA, UAG, UAA

This "dictionary" shows that there is no difficulty at all in translating from the four-letter alphabet of the nucleic acids to the twenty-letter alphabet of proteins. Indeed, there are quite a few more codons than are necessary—enough to give a number of the amino acids more than one codon of their own, and also enough to provide for starting and stopping signals for the protein chains. These signals are quite useful, for they permit a single messenger RNA molecule to carry the instructions for several different protein molecules, one after another. When the moving ribosome reaches a codon that signals Stop! it releases the growing protein chain. Then, when it comes to a starting signal, it begins to join amino acids together into a new protein chain.

Marshall Nirenberg, the Nobel Prize winner who first discovered that poly-U contains the code for polyphenylalanine, has reported on experiments that suggest that the genetic code works in exactly the same way for all the living creatures of our world, from bacteria up to man. Nirenberg and his research group mixed combinations of transfer RNA and amino acids taken from toads and from guinea pigs with ribosomes from a bacterium and messenger RNA molecules whose order of bases was known. The amino acids were lined up in the same way, no matter what organism the transfer RNA had come from.

And so the code of life, which holds the secrets of all our differences, also holds the answer to the many ways in which all forms of life are so very much alike.

How a Human Being Comes to Be

WHEN A HUMAN SPERM CELL MEETS AN EGG CELL, they join to form a single new cell that can become a baby. Inside a human sperm cell there is a set of 23 chromosomes—each a different kind. These chromosomes contain DNA. And as we know now, the DNA carries master plans for making a new human being. The egg cell has its own matching set of 23 chromosomes, its own set of master plans.

When an egg and a sperm join, they form a *zygote*, the first cell of a new human being. The two sets of chromosomes, 23 from each parent, are combined. The tiny zygote has two of each of the 23 kinds of chromosomes, just as every cell in your body does. With its complete set of chromosomes, containing the DNA with all the master plans that are needed, this single cell is ready to start a new bit of life on its way.

First the DNA makes more of itself. Each molecule makes a perfect copy of itself. This happens in much the same way that DNA makes RNA. The two strands of the double helix unzip, and nucleotides (combinations of an organic base, a sugar, and a phosphate) are lined up along the open edges. This time it is DNA nucleotides that are joined together, and new chains form along both of the old DNA strands. By the time the old molecule has finished unzipping, a new corresponding, or complementary strand has been added to each of the old chains of the original double helix. Now there are two complete DNA molecules instead of one. Each molecule contains one strand from the old DNA molecule and one new strand that has been built up, one nucleotide at a time, using the old strand as a pattern.

Fertilization, showing sperms and egg (top left), formation of the zygote (bottom left), and division of the zygote to form a new cell (bottom right).

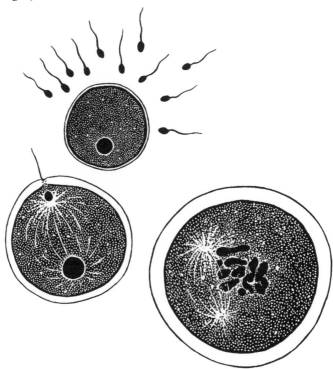

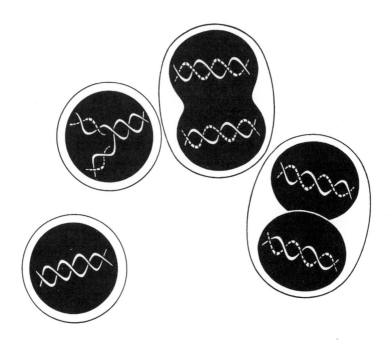

Cell division and duplication of DNA in egg cell.

Now the zygote has two sets of DNA, each exactly the same as the other. Soon the zygote divides in half, and there are two cells. Each receives one complete set of the DNA—23 pairs of chromosomes. In a while, the DNA molecules again make copies of themselves, and then the two cells split into four.

This happens again and again. Soon there are 8, 16, 32, and then 64 cells. At first all the cells are the same. But then they begin to differentiate. Soon there are brain cells and eye cells, and small buds that grow into arms and legs. Even a little tail begins to grow for a while and then disappears.

Day after day the unborn child grows bigger and bigger, and its cells become more and more different. This seems strange, indeed. For each cell has exactly the same set of DNA molecules, exactly the same set of plans.

How can this be? Scientists are not yet sure. They know that each cell uses only part of its plans. Eye cells make eyes, and not hair or feet. Stomach cells make the stomach, and not the heart or lungs. But though scientists know that this is so, they do not yet know how each cell knows just what part of its plans to use.

In the chromosomes the DNA is usually bound together with proteins, in combinations called *nucleoproteins*. It is believed that proteins called *histones* cover up nearly all the DNA and let only a small part stay free to work. The plans for eyes would be allowed to work in the eye cells. The plans for making a stomach, and then the plans for its work after the stomach has already been made, are left uncovered in the stomach cells.

Two French scientists, François Jacob and Jacques Monod, won a Nobel prize for figuring out how part of the DNA in a bacterium is turned on and off. They studied the portion of the DNA that carries the plans for three different enzymes. These enzymes work together to break down a sugar called *lactose*, which the bacterium uses for food.

The portion of DNA that carries the plans for making a particular protein is called a *gene*. This is the unit of heredity. Our chromosomes contain many thousands of different genes. Even the chromosome of a bacterium contains hundreds of genes. Each gene is many nucleotides long—usually more than a thousand.

The genes that make the three lactose-digesting enzymes in the bacterium are not always at work. They operate only when the sugar lactose is present. Jacob and Monod suggested that the work of the three genes is controlled by another, nearby gene. They named this gene a regulator and said that it carried the code for a special protein, called a repressor. The repressor protein could attach itself to the DNA molecule close to the three lactose genes and so repress them, or keep them from working. In this way, there would be an effective on-off switch, keeping the genes under control.

In 1966 molecular biologists at Harvard University isolated the repressor protein that Jacob and Monod had predicted. Another group found a similar repressor protein that works in a virus. Now scientists in many laboratories are at work studying how the repressor proteins and regulator genes work in microorganisms. They are especially eager to find out whether the genes in animals and man work in this way, too.

As the unborn child grows, one set of genes after another is uncovered in his DNA, transmits its plans, and then is covered up again when its work is done. After birth the DNA, the master planner, continues to work. As the child grows, his DNA is still telling his cells what to do—how much to grow, and how to work together to keep him well and strong. Even after the child becomes a man and stops growing, parts of his DNA are still at work. They direct the chemical activities of his trillions of cells and help make new cells to replace old ones that are damaged or wear out. Each new cell that is formed receives a copy of the same DNA, the same set of genes. And some of these genes may live on in his children and grandchildren.

Heredity and the World About Us

EVERY LIVING CREATURE ON THIS EARTH HAS ITS OWN special DNA. Each living thing has DNA molecules that are different from all the rest. That is why tigers and elephants, sunflowers and oak trees, and monkeys and people are all different.

If we look around us we can see that there are also great differences in people. Some are tall and some are short, some are thin and some fat. Some people have dark skins and others have light skins. Even in a single family there may be children with blond hair, red hair, and brown hair. A mother with blue eyes may have brown-eyed children. But if the father also has blue eyes, all of the children will have blue eyes.

Is there any reason for all this variety, or is nature just a big grab bag, where one never knows what is going to come out next? In a way this is true. One never knows for sure whether a baby is going to be a boy or a girl, until it is born. In many cases one cannot be sure what color eyes or hair it will have, or the shape of its nose. But often some pretty good guesses can be made. For scientists have found that there are definite rules of heredity: traits like hair color and eye color, the shape of the nose, and many other features are passed on from parents to children in a definite pattern.

The traits that make up a living organism, whether it is a bacterium or a sunflower or a man, are governed by the genes in its DNA. These genes carry the plans for protein molecules. Some proteins are building materials that help give shape to the body and its parts. Some proteins give color to eyes or hair. Many proteins are enzymes, which determine what other chemicals will be built up or broken down. Enzymes help us to breathe and to digest our food, to move, and all the other things our bodies must do to stay alive.

In man, and in most other animals and plants, there are two genes for each trait. One is found on each of a matching pair of chromosomes. One whole set of genes came from the mother, and the other whole set came from the father.

The pair of genes for a trait might be the same, or they might be different. For instance, if a boy has two genes for brown hair, he will be brown-haired. But what if he has one gene for brown hair and one gene for blond hair? He will still have brown hair.

How can this be? The brown hair gene seems to be much "stronger" than the blond hair gene. When the two are together in a pair, we see only the effects of the brown hair gene. Scientists say that brown hair is dominant to blond hair. No effects from the blond

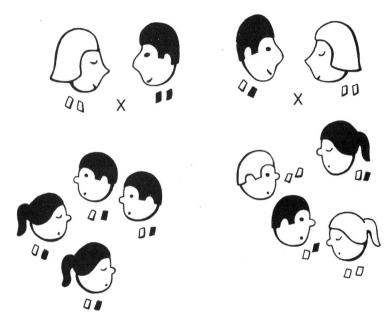

Hair colors to be expected from one blond-haired and one brown-haired parent.

hair gene can be seen unless both genes in the pair are blond hair genes. So it is clear that to be blond, a person must have two blond hair genes and no brown hair gene at all. That is why two blond-haired parents can have only blond children. For neither of them has any other kind of hair color genes to pass on to their children.

Geneticists—scientists who study heredity—call blond hair a recessive trait. The gene for blond hair never shows its effects unless there are two genes of the same kind.

It is *recessive* genes that make heredity so full of surprises. For a recessive gene stays hidden until it joins with another gene just like it. So if a brown-haired boy has a hidden blond hair gene, he may never know it. But if he grows up and marries a blonde girl, some of their children may be blond. For he will give each child half of his DNA—one set of his genes. His wife will provide the other set. But all her hair genes will be blond. So any child that happens to get the father's blond hair gene will be blond, and any child that happens to get his brown hair gene will be brown-haired.

All of our traits are inherited in this way. But often more than one set of genes helps to control a trait. Geneticists have found about ten different pairs of genes controlling skin color. That is why there are so many shades of skin color, from very pale to very dark. Eye color, too, is actually controlled by many genes although blue eyes are always recessive. So are height and intelligence. Even hair color is controlled by more than a single pair of genes. That is why people can have different shades of hair, from a blond so pale it is almost white to a brown or orangy red, all the way to the darkest black.

But even though there are many differences from person to person, cat to cat, and tree to tree, each living creature is very much like the others of its kind. Both the differences and the similarities are coded in DNA, the amazing chemical that determines what we are and what our children will be.

When the Code
Goes Wrong

THE DNA IN EACH CELL IN YOUR BODY CONTAINS A fantastic amount of information. If all this information could be recorded on paper, there would be enough to fill a thousand books with 500 pages in each. New cells are being formed in your body all the time. Each of these cells contains the same set of plans or DNA. For when one cell divides to form two new ones, its DNA is copied, so that there are two identical sets, one for each daughter cell.

The copying of DNA in the cell is amazingly accurate. If you copied ten pages from a book and made only one mistake, you would be doing very well. But a cell makes only about one mistake in every *million* pages when it duplicates its DNA.

When the parent cell makes one of these rare errors in copying its DNA, a daughter cell will have a set of DNA that is slightly different from those of the other cells. Such a change in the DNA is called a *mutation*.

The "fancy" goldfish shown at the top is a mutant.

The daughter cell will pass on the mutation to its own daughters when it divides, and they may pass it on in turn.

Mutations are changes in the plans that the DNA carries. If a mutation occurs in one of the early cells that starts off the life of a new baby, the plans of development may be terribly upset. The baby might grow two heads, or no arms, or only a single eye in the middle of its forehead. Each year a quarter of a million American babies are born deformed in some major way. It is believed that most of these deformities result from mutations in the DNA.

There are thousands of diseases that are caused by mutations. In most of these cases the changed DNA cannot direct the making of some important chemical that the body needs. For example, each year about 400 babies in the United States are born with a disease called phenylketonuria (PKU). The name of the disease comes from the fact that a compound called phenylketone is found in their urine. This substance is not usually found in the urine of normal people, because their bodies contain a certain enzyme that breaks down the phenylketone into other substances. This enzyme is missing in the bodies of people with PKU—the part of their DNA that holds the plans for making it has mutated, so that it does not work properly.

If doctors do not realize right away that a baby has PKU, it may become mentally retarded. But if they catch it in time, they can feed the baby a special diet, and it will grow up to be normal and healthy. In many hospitals, the urine of all the newborn babies is tested for phenylketone to discover any infants suffering from PKU while there is still time to treat the disease.

Mutations thus can have many serious effects. But actually most mutations are not serious at all. Indeed, scientists believe that everyone has at least one mutation, and probably many more. For the most part, these mutations are so minor that we never even notice them. For example, perhaps one of the cells in your skin has just mutated. The chances are very small that this mutation will ever produce a change that you can detect. First of all, since the DNA in each cell is a complete set, most of it does not have anything to do with the growth and work of the skin. The genes for the color of the eyes, the enzymes that help digest our food, the oxygen-carrying chemicals in the blood, and an enormous variety of others are all "turned off" in skin cells. They do not work there. If a mutation occurs in any of these genes, it will not have any effect at all. Even if the mutation does occur in a gene in the working part of the DNA, you still might completely miss its effects. A single skin cell is very tiny, so small that you would need a microscope to see it. Perhaps the mutation might cause it to make more or less of the brown pigment melanin, and thus form a tiny dot of a different color from the rest of the skin. But would you notice such a tiny dot at all? Perhaps the skin cell was one that normally would produce a small hair, and the mutation prevented its formation. You would not be very likely to realize that one small hair was missing from your arm or body.

If the mutated skin cell were one that divides to form new skin cells, it could pass its changed gene on to new generations of cells. Eventually a little group of cells would be formed, many of them carrying the same mutation. Then you might notice a small freckle or mole, or a patch of skin without any hair. If the mutation was the kind that makes a cell keep on growing and dividing, even when normal skin cells would stop, it could grow into a cancer!

Most of the mutations that occur happen in body cells. They are called *somatic mutations*, from the word *soma*, which means body. Their effects are usually very minor. Indeed, since many types of cells in the body do not divide any more once a person is fully grown, or divide only very slowly, the mutation may have its effects on only a single cell.

But the body also contains a certain number of reproductive or germ cells. These are the cells that form the eggs or sperms that may one day join with another reproductive cell to start the life of a new organism. Mutations in the germ cells are called *genetic* mutations. They are the cause of many birth defects. For after an egg and a sperm join, and a new organism begins to develop, sets of plans in the DNA are turned on one after another. If any of these plans has been changed by a mutation, the new organism will not develop normally.

How do mutations happen? During the lifetime of a cell and during its division to form two daughter cells, there are many chances for things to go wrong. For example, when the DNA of the cell is copied, there are then two complete sets of chromosomes, one a duplicate of the other. The next step is for the pairs of "identical twin" chromosomes to separate, so that each daughter cell will receive one of each and thus have a full set of its own. Nearly always this works smoothly. But once in awhile, the chromosomes are not evenly divided. One daughter cell receives both of a particular kind, while the other daughter cell does not get any of that kind at all. Both the cells now have a changed set of chromosomes—one has too many, and the other does not have enough.

Another type of chromosome mutation occurs when the DNA is copied and then duplicated again before the cell divides. In this case the two daughter cells each have twice as many chromosomes as they should.

Sometimes chromosomes break apart. The cell contains special "DNA-joining enzymes," which can put the broken pieces back together. In this way many changes that would have been mutations are repaired before they can have any effects. But sometimes the pieces are not joined back together in the same way they were before. Perhaps a chunk of broken DNA may be dropped out of the middle of a chromosome when broken ends are joined together. A broken piece from one chromosome may be accidentally added onto the end of a different chromosome. Or two broken parts of a chromosome may be joined with the wrong ends together, so that one part of the chromosome is lined up backwards.

These chromosome mutations may be caused by various things, such as heat, certain chemicals, X-rays, and the ultraviolet radiations from the sun. These influences are all around us, and they are producing changes in our DNA all the time. Most of the time, the cell can repair the damage very quickly, before a mutation can result. For usually only one of the strands of DNA is broken. The other strand holds the broken pieces in place, and they are neatly repaired by the DNA-joining enzymes of the cell. It is mainly when there are double breaks, on both of the DNA chains, that chromosome mutations occur.

In addition to breaks in the chromosomes, some chemicals and radiations can also produce changes in the genes themselves, in the bases of the DNA. For example, scientists have made a compound called 5-bromouracil (BU), which is very much like thymine (T). If BU is added when DNA is being made, the cell may build this chemical into the DNA molecule, substituting it for T. But 5-bromouracil is not exactly

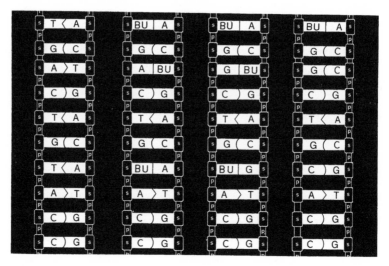

Mutation of DNA through the substitution of BU for T. The T becomes C. And a "word" that might have been CTG becomes CCG.

like thymine. When the changed DNA is being copied, a mistake may be made. Instead of an adenine (A), the BU may be paired up with a guanine (G). When this new chain, in turn, is used as a pattern, the chain of bases that is built up will contain a cytosine (C), where there should have been a thymine. Now the "code" of DNA has been completely changed. Perhaps the three-letter "word" was originally A-T-G. When BU was added, it became A-BU-G, but then the copy errors changed it into A-C-G.

A substance that causes mutations is called a *mutagen*. Some of the chemical mutagens, like BU, are very similar to the normal bases of DNA and can be built into its chains. Others, such as a compound called nitrous acid, act on the bases in the nucleic acid and change them chemically so that they no longer pair up in the same way. Then, as the DNA is copied and recopied, the code is changed.

When the Code Goes Wrong

The code of life contains the blueprints for all the daily activities of living organisms. A plant turns its leaves toward the sun, manufactures its own food from simple chemicals, and forms flowers and seeds that will produce the new generation. An animal finds food and digests it, tries to avoid its enemies, moves about from place to place, and eventually it may mate and raise its young. All these activities usually work fairly well, for the animals and plants that exist in our world today are the newest generation of family groups whose history goes back for millions of years. The kinds of animals and plants that were not successful in the daily fight for life have died out and vanished from the earth. Since the cell's activities, directed by DNA, normally run so smoothly, you might expect that most changes in the code would not be improvements—and this indeed is so.

Most mutations either are so slight that they do not seem to have much effect on an organism's chance to survive, or they harm it in some way. A fruit fly, for example, that had orange eyes instead of the normal red ones, would probably be able to get along just as well as if it had not had the mutation. But if a mutation caused a fruit fly to be born without any eyes at all, it would probably mean an early death for the unlucky mutant. It would not be able to see to find its food or avoid its enemies. (Scientists have seen just such mutations in their studies of fruit flies in the laboratory.)

Every now and then, however, a mutation occurs that actually helps an organism to survive. Perhaps it can run or fly faster than the others of its kind. Or it may have skin or fur that matches the background of the place where it lives, so that it can remain hidden from its enemies. Perhaps it has more offspring or can care for them better, so that more of them survive. Scientists believe that the enormous variety of creatures that inhabit the earth today all came from a common ancestor. Over billions of years, many mutations appeared in the descendants of these long-ago ancestors. Some mutations—a very few—permitted certain creatures to adapt better to the conditions of a particular environment, and these creatures survived and passed on their valuable mutations to their offspring.

Even today, farmers and animal breeders watch for the small number of beneficial mutations that pop up from time to time and use them to breed stronger and better plants and animals. Among other things, they are breeding strains of corn with more nourishing protein and rice that gives a much higher yield per acre.

Knowledge
from the Culture Dish

IF YOU WANTED TO STUDY HEREDITY AND HOW THE
code of life is passed on from one generation to another, you would have to work with living things.
What would be the best kind to choose? People? They
take too long to grow up, and they have only one or
two babies at a time. Mice would be better, for they
can have offspring when they are only a couple of
months old, and they can have as many as a dozen at
a time. Mice are used in genetics experiments, but there
are even better organisms for these studies.

What about plants? The father of genetics, Gregor
Mendel, used garden peas in his experiments; each seed
grew into a plant with many pods and more than a
hundred seeds. Mendel was able to study many thousands of plants, and he discovered important facts
about how traits are passed on from parents to offspring through many generations. But working with
peas and other plants can take years, and you need a

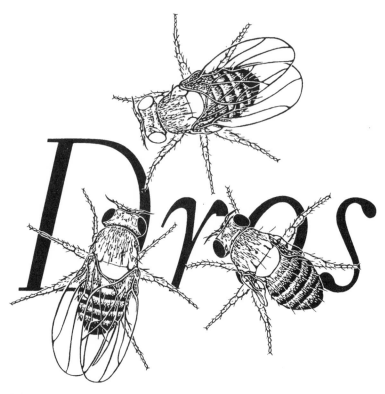

Of these three fruit flies, two are mutants. The top has white eyes and the one at the bottom right has only vestigial wings. The text type of this book is blown up to the same size as the fruit flies in this illustration.

field to grow them. The next big advance in genetics did not come until scientists found a better organism to study: the fruit fly.

Fruit flies can have about 200 offspring at a time, and the new babies are fully grown and ready to mate and lay eggs of their own after only about ten days. They can be kept in little bottles on a laboratory shelf. The great American geneticist Thomas Morgan worked with fruit flies for many years. The wild fruit flies that he started with had black bodies and red eyes. But as he mated pair after pair and examined thousands and thousands of offspring, he found a few that were different. Now and then there was a fruit fly with white eyes or brown eyes or apricot-colored eyes. Some had light-colored bodies or wings that were shorter than usual or curled in a curious way. Morgan saved all these different fruit flies and studied how the mutations they carried were passed on from generation to generation. From these studies he gained many new ideas about how the chromosomes and the smaller units within them—the genes—must work.

Another geneticist, H. J. Muller, tried treating fruit flies with X-rays. He discovered that these radiations caused mutations of the same kind that Morgan had found, but the changes occurred a hundred times as often. X-rays gave geneticists an important new tool for studying heredity—the ability to make changes in the chromosomes and watch their effects.

But even the fruit fly is not the best organism for studying the chromosomes themselves. Our knowledge of the chemicals that carry the code of life was not gained until scientists turned to still smaller creatures— microorganisms.

One of the microorganisms that has become a "geneticist's pet" is the red bread mold, *Neurospora crassa*. It is easy to raise and has given a wealth of information about heredity. This mold forms a fuzzy reddish growth on old bread. Under a microscope, it can be seen that it is made up of many long, branching chains that look like strings of oval-shaped beads.

Many types of bacteria are also used in modern genetics experiments. Some cause disease in humans or animals, such as the tiny round forms that cause pneumonia. Others are bacteria that are normally found in people's intestines. One of these is a rod-shaped bacterium called *Escherichia coli*. This bacterium is studied all over the world, and thousands of reports have been written about it. Scientists do not like to bother with long names any more than other people do, and they usually abbreviate it as *E. coli*.

Bacteria can be grown in the laboratory in several convenient ways. They can be grown in test tubes or in low, flat-bottomed glass dishes in a watery broth made by cooking meat or fish or corn. Or a jelly-like substance called *agar* may be poured into dishes or slanted test tubes. Food substances and other chemicals may be added to this culture medium, and the bacteria grow on the surface of the solid jelly. (The test tubes are slanted so that there will be a larger surface for the bacteria to grow on.)

Bacteria multiply amazingly fast. When a bacterium is fully grown and ready to reproduce, it copies its DNA and then divides in two. Each daughter cell receives a complete set of DNA, and the two new cells begin to grow until they too are ready to divide. A new generation of bacteria can be formed in as little as 20 or 30 minutes. And so, starting with a single bacterium, a geneticist may have millions to work with in just a few hours.

A single bacterium is so small that it can be seen only with a very good microscope. But when bacteria grow together by the millions, they form colonies that can be seen even without a magnifying glass. These colonies have a very definite size and shape, depending on the conditions and on the type of bacteria forming them. Some colonies look like tiny round

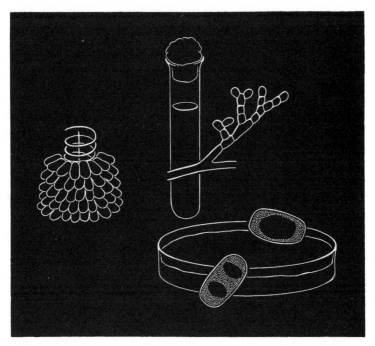

Colony shapes for three common bacteria: left, tobacco mosaic virus; top center, *Neurospora;* bottom, *E. coli.*

buttons, scattered over the culture dish. Others may be large and lacy. Some are chalky white or pearly or bright colored.

Each colony growing on a culture dish was formed from the descendants of a single bacterium. All of the individuals that make up the colony have exactly the same heredity, for each has received a copy of the DNA of the original parent. The geneticist can scrape off a single colony and transfer it to a new dish or a test tube of broth. Then he will have a whole population of bacteria to work with, all with the same heredity. A population of this kind, all descended from a single parent, is called a *clone.*

Working with a clone of bacteria is much less confusing than working with groups of mice or fruit flies. Mice and fruit flies get their chromosomes from two parents, and even brothers and sisters can have quite different sets of DNA.

The geneticist can conduct many interesting kinds of experiments with clones of bacteria. He may treat them with radiations or chemicals. Most of the bacteria will be killed, but among those that remain, there will be many with mutations. Perhaps a mutated bacterium will now be unable to make a certain chemical that it needs to grow. It will not be able to survive and give rise to colonies unless this chemical is added to the agar or broth in which it is growing. A mutation may cause a change in the shape or color of the colonies that bacteria form. It may make them unable to infect an animal in which they caused diseases before the mutation. Some mutations make bacteria able to survive even when penicillin or other antibiotics are added to the medium. Such mutations sometimes occur in natural populations of disease germs. They produce diseases that are resistant to antibiotics and may cause difficult problems for doctors who are trying to treat the patients.

Now that scientists are beginning to study the chemistry of DNA to determine how its bases are arranged, they are matching changes in the DNA to the changes in the behavior and appearance of bacteria and their colonies. Gradually they are learning more and more about the code of life.

Indeed, the part that DNA plays in heredity was first discovered in experiments on bacteria. An English researcher, Fred Griffith, tried injecting two types of pneumococci, bacteria that cause pneumonia, into mice at the same time. One type of pneumococci could make mice ill, while the other type was a form that did not have any apparent effects. Griffith killed the virulent bacteria (those that could give the mice pneumonia) by heating them before he injected them. Yet he found that the mice got pneumonia anyway. What could be causing the disease? It could not be the killed bacteria, and the other type had never caused any trouble when it was injected by itself. When Griffith took samples of bacteria from the blood of the mice and grew them in a culture medium, he found that the harmless bacteria had somehow been transformed into a type very similar to the virulent one.

Now scientists in many laboratories began to search for the "transforming principle" that had changed the bacteria so dramatically. Finally, in 1944, a research team announced that it was DNA from the dead bacteria that changed the heredity of the living form.

Bacteria are so small that they cannot be seen without a good microscope. But scientists have discovered another group of microorganisms so small that they cannot be seen at all, even with the best of the ordinary microscopes. These are the viruses, and they can be seen only with an electron microscope.

There are many kinds of viruses. Some are shaped like tiny balls or cubes or rods, or even like a miniature tadpole with a head and a long tail. Some viruses cause diseases in humans and other animals. Colds, influenza, and smallpox are all caused by viruses. Some viruses cause diseases in plants. An important one of this type is the tobacco mosaic virus, which causes spots to form on tobacco leaves. Some viruses even infect bacteria. These viruses are called *bacteriophages* (which means "bacteria-eaters"), or *phages* for short.

All these different kinds of viruses are built in basically the same way. Inside are strands of nucleic acids —either DNA or RNA, but not both—neatly folded. This core of nucleic acids is wrapped in a coat made of protein units, arranged in a regular pattern. The simplest viruses contain only these two parts and nothing more. But some viruses contain other chemicals in addition: proteins, fatty substances, carbohydrates, and even vitamins and tiny bits of metals.

When a virus infects an animal or plant or bacterium, the virus nucleic acid enters the cell of its host, leaving the protein coat behind. In some way that scientists do not yet completely understand, the virus nucleic acid forces the host cell to begin manufacturing new virus particles. The genes of the virus are used as the pattern, and the cell becomes a factory, mass-producing virus nucleic acids and proteins by the hundreds. The parts of the new viruses are put together, and they leave the cell, ready to infect new cells.

Viruses are such simple forms of life that they are almost like naked genes. For this reason they are almost ideal subjects for geneticists who want to study how the chemicals of the code of life work. For example, they have learned to take apart the RNA and the protein coat of the tobacco mosaic virus and put them back together. They have even taken the protein coat from one kind of tobacco mosaic virus and combined it with the RNA of another kind. The hybrid virus that they obtained was able to infect tobacco plants and reproduce itself, but the new virus offspring that were formed were just like the original parent

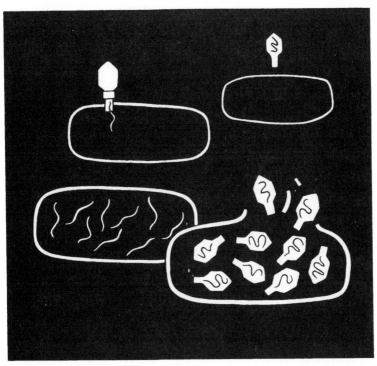

A phage approaches a normal cell, leaves its protein coat behind, and enters the cell, forcing the cell to manufacture new phages, which leave to infect other cells.

kind from which the RNA was taken. In this way the scientists received more evidence that it is the nucleic acid, not the protein, that carries the information of heredity.

Researchers have also learned how the chemicals that form the protein coat of tobacco mosaic virus are put together, and they have mapped out much of its RNA. Now they are using chemicals that change definite parts of the RNA and observing the changes that occur in the protein that is made with the mutated RNA as a pattern. In this way they are learning more about the workings of the code of life.

Geneticists are also studying phages, the viruses that infect bacteria. Phages are generally shaped like tadpoles, with long tails. The tail attaches to the outer wall of a bacterium and makes a sort of chemical glue that helps it to stick fast. Then special enzymes made by the phage dissolve a hole in the bacterium's outer wall, and the phage nucleic acid slips through, almost as if it were being injected with a hypodermic needle. The empty protein coat of the phage is left behind, sticking to the outer wall. Inside the cell of the bacterium, the virus may remain quietly, apparently doing nothing. Or it may spark a flurry of furious activity. New phage particles are manufactured, and then the bacterium bursts, dumping out the phages. When this occurs among bacteria growing in a culture dish or in a test tube, clear spots are formed among the colonies of bacteria. In these clear spots, which are called *plaques*, the bacteria have been killed by the infecting phages.

Phages may be very simple organisms, but they do have a number of characteristics that are inherited through plans carried in their nucleic acid. Their size and shape, the kinds of bacteria they infect, and the kinds of plaques they form, can all be studied by geneticists. Other viruses, too, have inherited characteristics that geneticists can study.

Viruses can also change the heredity of the host cells that they infect. Part of the virus nucleic acid may be added to the genes of the cell. These will be passed on to its descendants when it divides. Many researchers now believe that this is a way in which cancer cells may be formed. They have taken apart the double strands of DNA of viruses suspected of causing cancer and matched them with the genes of cancer cells. If the virus genes were "hiding" inside the cells, they would zip up together with one of the separated strands of virus DNA. And that is exactly what happened. DNA that "matched" the virus DNA was found among the chromosomes of the cell.

The same kind of technique was recently used to make a discovery that surprised and excited geneticists: it was found that sometimes the genetic code can work backward! Normally DNA reproduces itself and also serves as a pattern for various kinds of RNA, which in turn make proteins. But what about RNA viruses, which do not have any DNA at all? The geneticist Sol Spiegelman discovered some enzymes in these viruses that help RNA to reproduce itself, just as DNA does in normal cells. Since this virus RNA could reproduce itself, and could also serve as a pattern for making proteins, viruses could thus get along without any DNA very nicely. But some RNA viruses can cause tumors in animals. In 1964, Howard Temin suggested that the RNA in these viruses could serve as a pattern for making DNA! Most researchers laughed at the idea. After all, everyone knew that DNA makes RNA, and not the other way around. Dr. Temin kept working and found more evidence for his theory, which he announced at a conference in 1970. Sol Spiegelman was so impressed with Temin's report that he went back to his laboratory and began experiments of his own. Soon he found that eight different RNA viruses that cause cancer in animals can force the cells they infect to form matching DNA. This DNA stays inside the cells, and they and their descendants become cancer cells. Spiegelman also tested four RNA viruses that do not cause cancers, and he found that they do not produce DNA.

Viruses can leave some of their own genes behind in a cell and transform a normal cell into a cancer cell. But they can also carry genes from a host cell out with them and transfer them to a new host cell. The new cell now has "inherited" some characteristics from the host that the virus had infected before. This has been observed many times in bacteria infected by phages, and in virus-infected plants and animals, too. If the genes that the virus brings along are harmful ones, the new host may grow ill and die. But what if "good" genes could be attached to a harmless virus and introduced into the cell? Perhaps the health of the host could be improved. This is one technique that scientists are hoping to use in the exciting new field of genetic engineering.

Genes in the Laboratory

GENES CARRY THE BLUEPRINTS FOR LIFE. AS EACH CREA-
ture grows—whether it is a human or an animal, a
plant, or a microorganism too tiny to be seen—each step
of the way it follows the set of plans "written" in a
chemical code in its DNA. Some genes, parts of the
DNA strand, determine how many legs a creature
will have, or whether it will have eyes and nose and
mouth, and what color and shape parts of the creature
will have. Some genes make important proteins that
help to keep the body healthy, such as the hemoglobin
in the blood that carries oxygen to the body cells, and
enzymes in the mouth, stomach, and intestines that
help to digest food. There are even genes that make
special enzymes that help the cells to make new genes!

The genes, which carry the code of life, are so important that thousands of scientists are devoting their
lives to finding out more about them and how they
work. They are making exciting progress. Indeed, in

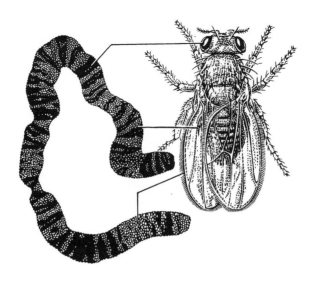

A fruit fly with one of its chromosomes, showing areas in chromosome that control development of specific parts of the fly.

the last dozen years or so, more Nobel Prizes have been awarded to geneticists than to scientists in any other field. At the beginning of the century, geneticists could study only the effects of the genes—the patterns of heredity and changes caused by mutations. But today's geneticists are getting down to the core of heredity, studying the very chemicals of the code of life.

Recently two of the most exciting events of all have been announced. Scientists have actually isolated and looked at a single gene, just 0.000055 of an inch long. And another group of researchers has made a gene in the laboratory, built up from simple chemicals.

It may seem surprising that the first single gene was not isolated until November 1969, even though Watson and Crick had proposed their double helix model of DNA back in 1953, and Nirenberg and Ochoa cracked the genetic code in 1961. Researchers had taken DNA strands apart and put them back together;

they had made artificial nucleic acids in the laboratory; they had used DNA from microorganisms as patterns to build up matching RNA molecules and even a complete new set of DNA of a phage. All this was accomplished before the first single gene was isolated.

Yet this task was more complicated than it might seem. Just what is a gene, after all? When scientists first looked at chromosomes under a microscope, they noticed that these structures looked very much like strings of beads. Then the name *gene* was invented for the unit of heredity—the part of a chromosome that carries the plans for one particular trait, such as the color of hair, or the protein that our fingernails are made of. Since the chromosomes are made up of long series of genes, and they look like strings of beads under a microscope, everyone thought that each "bead" must be a gene. But then, as researchers learned more about the chromosomes and genes, and began to match particular parts of the chromosomes to particular traits, they found that things were not so simple. Sometimes the genes for several different traits all seemed to be in one "bead" of a chromosome. As more was learned about the chemistry of the chromosomes, scientists realized that genes are portions of the DNA double chains, perhaps a hundred, a thousand, or even several thousand bases long.

Much has been learned about the genes attached to other genes in chromosomes. But scientists could learn much more about how a gene works, and especially how it is turned on and off, if they could work with only one gene, without all the others around to confuse things.

A research team at Harvard Medical School, led by Dr. Jonathan Beckwith, thought of a way to isolate a single gene. They worked with a bacterium, the intestinal bacterium *E. coli*, and two different phages. Both these phages can infect *E. coli*, but they do not cause the bacterium to manufacture new phage particles and then burst apart. Instead, the virus DNA attaches itself to the DNA of the bacterium, remains quietly there for awhile, and then leaves. When the phages leave the bacterium, they carry away some of its genes, along with their own.

Beckwith's team picked two viruses that carry away different sets of genes, with only one *E. coli* gene in common. This gene is called the *lac* gene, because it makes an enzyme that breaks down the sugar *lac*tose into simpler substances that the bacterium can use for energy.

The experiment was a very clever one. First *E. coli* bacteria were infected with one of the phages. Then another sample of bacteria was infected with the other phage. Now the researchers had two different phages that were carrying genes from the bacterium. Working with each sample separately, they carefully took apart the double strands of the phage DNA. Then they mixed one of the strands from one phage with the proper DNA strand from the other phage. If the two strands matched, their bases would pair up, and they would coil up into a double helix. But the two strands had come from two different phages, with different collections of genes. The only part that matched was the one lac gene that both phages had carried away from *E. coli*. This portion of the two DNA strands

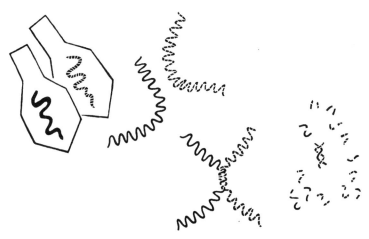

The Beckwith phage experiment: 1. two phages with *E. coli* genes; 2. separated DNA strands; 3. the joined gene; 4. a single gene surrounded by unmatching strands.

did indeed coil up into a double helix, leaving the rest of the DNA dangling in separate strands at each end.

Now the Beckwith team added a special chemical that breaks up single-strand nucleic acids, but leaves double-strand DNA alone. All the single strands that did not match were dissolved away, and only the lac gene remained.

Not long after the first gene was isolated, in the middle of 1970, the Nobel Prize winner Har Gobind Khorana announced that he had synthesized a gene in the laboratory. Scientists had been trying to make nucleic acids for many years. Indeed, the 1959 Nobel Prize in physiology and medicine was awarded to two geneticists, Severo Ochoa and Arthur Kornberg, for their work in this field.

In 1955, Dr. Ochoa discovered an enzyme that made nucleoside diphosphates (combinations of a nitrogen base, a ribose sugar, and two phosphate groups) link up together to form a sort of RNA. This reaction took place even in a test tube, without any living organism.

Ochoa's achievement was a very important step forward in learning about the chemical code of life. Indeed, this Nobel Prize winner used the reaction he had studied to make a number of kinds of artificial RNA and then studied the kinds of proteins that were made, using his artificial RNA molecules as the set of plans. These were the experiments that helped Ochoa crack the code of life.

But important as Severo Ochoa's experiments were, he did not really synthesize chemicals of life. For the RNA molecules that he made were put together randomly, that is, the nucleosides were lined up in no particular order, just as they happened to come together. But in the DNA and RNA of living organisms, the order of the nucleosides is all important—it is the order of the bases in the genes that determines whether the zygote of a living organism will develop into a cat or a caterpillar, a tulip or a man.

Two years after Severo Ochoa discovered his RNA-synthesizing enzyme, another geneticist, Arthur Kornberg, found an enzyme that living creatures use to make DNA. He called this enzyme DNA *polymerase*. (A *polymer* is a very large molecule made of many units joined together. DNA and RNA are polymers; so are proteins, starch, and the cellulose found in plant cells. Chemists have also made many synthetic polymers, such as nylon and artificial rubber.)

Kornberg isolated his DNA polymerase from cells of *E. coli*. This bacterium can grow and reproduce in only 20 minutes, so that its cells are continually making new DNA. When Kornberg added his enzyme to a mixture of nucleoside triphosphates (nitrogen base and deoxyribose sugar with three phosphate groups joined together), they formed molecules of DNA. But this reaction took place in a test tube only if some DNA taken from some living organism was also present. The readymade DNA was used as a pattern or template, and the new DNA that was formed was found to be a copy of it.

In 1967, Kornberg announced that he had made a whole chromosome of a phage in a test tube. The phage, called *PhiX174*, has a very simple chromosome: just one strand, about 6000 bases long, joined in a circle. Kornberg isolated the phage DNA and used it as the template for synthesizing a new DNA ring. This new ring was marked in a very interesting and useful way. For instead of adding thymine, Kornberg used the compound 5-bromouracil. This nitrogen base pairs up in the same way that thymine does, but it is heavier. And so the new DNA ring, in which all the places that should be occupied by thymines were taken up by 5-bromouracils instead, was also heavier than the original phage DNA.

Now Kornberg broke the two rings apart and separated them in a high-speed centrifuge. Have you ever swung a bucket of water around on a rope? If you were careful, none of the water spilled out—it was kept in the moving bucket by centrifugal force. In a centrifuge, tubes with mixtures of chemical substances are spun about at very high speeds. Centrifugal force makes the solid particles move away from the center of the circle. The amount that they move depends on how heavy they are. When the centrifuge stops, the heaviest particles are at the bottom of the tubes, the

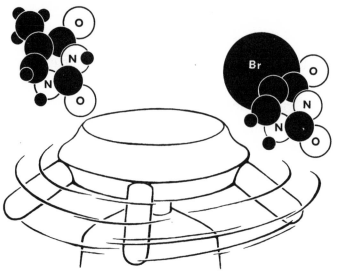

The Kornberg experiment: A centrifuge with diagrams showing the heavier phage molecule with 5-bromouracil and the lighter with thymines.

next heaviest a little farther up, and so on. By substituting 5-bromouracil for thymine in the DNA that he made, Kornberg was able to make the weights of the two rings different enough so that they could be nicely separated by centrifuging.

After he had the two rings separated, Kornberg tested the one he had made for biological activity. That is, he tested it to see if it would behave as a normal phage chromosome does, and direct bacterial cells to make more phage particles. It did indeed—it was real DNA, even though it had 5-bromouracil in place of thymine.

But perhaps a mistake had been made. Perhaps a bit of the original phage DNA had sneaked through, and that was what was active. Kornberg could not be sure, so he took his experiments one step further. He used his heavy DNA as a template and made another ring of phage DNA, this time using thymine in his mixture of raw materials. This new DNA turned out to be active too, and it was exactly like the original phage DNA—just as it should be.

Arthur Kornberg's announcement caused great excitement. President Lyndon Johnson called the work "an awesome achievement" and said that Kornberg's team had "unlocked a fundamental secret of life." Some enthusiastic scientists described the achievement as "the synthesis of life." It was not really a synthesis of life, though. For a ready-made DNA template was needed to be copied, and indeed, the DNA that was made was an unusually simple kind—only a single strand, instead of the double-strand form that all higher organisms have in their cells. No one yet had mixed simple chemicals in the laboratory and made a real gene.

That was what Har Gobind Khorana finally accomplished in 1970. Dr. Khorana also worked with a microorganism, in this case yeast cells. Other scientists had figured out the order of the nitrogen bases in one of the kinds of RNA of these cells, the transfer RNA that picks up the amino acid alanine and brings it to the ribosomes to be built into the proteins of the yeast cell. The genetic code had already been broken, and it was known that each kind of RNA is made on a DNA template, copying off the pattern stored in the genes. It was not too hard, therefore, to work backward from the RNA sequence to figure out what the DNA strand that it was copied from must be like. And once that one strand was known, the other was known too. For the bases of DNA always pair in the same way: wherever there is an adenine in one strand, there must be a thymine in the matching strand, a guanine corresponding to a cytosine, and so on. Soon Khorana had a map on paper—the order of the nucleotides in the gene that he was going to synthesize. It would be the gene for making alanine transfer RNA, and it was only 77 nucleotides long. But how was he going to make it? He did not want to use a ready-made template, as Kornberg had done. He wanted to synthesize the whole gene. But although scientists had worked out some ways to link nucleotides together, these were good only for short polymers, up to about 20 nucleotides long.

Dr. Khorana used an enzyme that had been discovered not too long before. It is called DNA-joining enzyme. Inside the cell, it is used to repair DNA strands that have broken accidentally. If one strand is still whole, the two broken ends can be matched up against it and held in place while the DNA-joining enzyme "glues" them together again. Arthur Kornberg used the DNA-joining enzyme when he synthesized his phage chromosome. After the whole chromosome had been built up, it was in the form of a long chain, and in that form it did not work as a chromosome at all. The DNA-joining enzyme joined the two ends of the chain together to form the circle that was biologically active.

Using the DNA-joining enzyme, Har Gobind Khorana worked out a new way to build up double-strand DNA molecules, which he calls the "sticky end" technique. He started out by making two short chains of nucleotides, carefully following the blueprint for the yeast alanine transfer RNA gene. One of the chains consisted of bases 21 to 40 of one strand of the DNA.

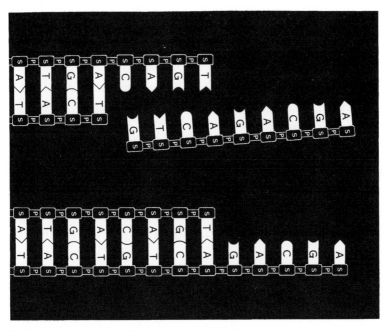

Khorana's "sticky-end" technique for making a gene.

The other chain contained bases 31 to 50 of the other strand. When he mixed the two together, the portions corresponding to bases 31 to 40 matched perfectly; chemical bonds formed between the pairs of bases, and these portions coiled up together. But there was a part of each chain that did not match: bases 21 to 30 on one chain and 41 to 50 on the other. These two single strands dangled free at the ends of the double stranded portion. They were the "sticky ends." Now Khorana made another single chain of nucleotides. Part of it corresponded perfectly to one of the "sticky ends," but it was longer. When this new chain was added, the matching bases paired up, leaving a new "sticky end" dangling. The DNA-joining enzyme linked up the two parts of the chain, which were held together on the complementary strand. Now the process was repeated again and again at both ends of the chain, joining new chains to the sticky ends, until the gene was complete. A whole gene had been made in the laboratory, from mixtures of nucleotides, without using the DNA from any living thing as a model to copy.

The yeast alanine transfer RNA gene is a very small gene, but its synthesis is an important beginning. The same methods that were used to make it can also be used to make larger genes, perhaps even human genes. Now that scientists are learning to make genes in the laboratory, they are growing more and more excited about what can be done with them. Man is gaining the power to change his own heredity.

Genetic Engineering
and Other New Frontiers

IN JUNE OF 1970, A NOBEL PRIZE-WINNING GENETICIST, Joshua Lederberg, testified before a Congressional committee. This was the committee in charge of recommending what money should be spent for medical research, and Dr. Lederberg was asking for a great deal of money—ten million dollars! The money would be used to form a genetics study group to coordinate research in genetics so that new results could be used more quickly to help people, and also to support many new and important research projects in genetics. At least a quarter of all the people in hospitals and institutions, Dr. Lederberg pointed out, are suffering from hereditary diseases—mistakes in their genes that can result in mental retardation, crippling, or even death. As we learn more about the code of life and how to fix genes when the code goes wrong, we will be able to save many wasted lives.

Congress passed the ten million dollar appropriation

that Dr. Lederberg asked for, and a "genetics task force" was formed. This is just one indication of how important the study of the code of life is becoming in our world. Now that scientists have synthesized a gene, geneticists are dreaming of working with the chemicals of life, correcting errors and perhaps even improving our heredity. This growing new science has been named genetic engineering.

One of the important stepping-stones to a real, working science of genetic engineering is the ability to make changes in the genes, to turn genes on and off, and even to synthesize new genes—perhaps ones that have never existed before. With the work of Kornberg, Khorana, and an army of other geneticists, scientists are learning to do all these things. But another important step is to be able to get new genes into the cells, where they can do their work. A gene in a test tube will not be of much help in curing diseases.

Curiously enough, progress along this line was made long before there seemed to be much hope for using it. Genetic engineers are looking to viruses as helpers in their work.

You have probably suffered from a number of virus diseases: colds, and perhaps influenza, chicken pox, measles, or mumps. Some viruses are also suspected of being causes of cancer. Yet not all viruses cause diseases. And many of them have what may be a very useful ability: they can enter a cell and attach their nucleic acid to its genes, and perhaps even be passed on to its offspring. If a particular virus has some desirable genes of its own, or if new genes, made in the laboratory, can be added to it, it may be used to correct or improve a person's own genes.

One of the most active workers in this field is Stanfield Rogers, at the Oak Ridge National Laboratory in Tennessee. He has made chemical changes in virus DNA and then used the virus to bring new genes into plants. Another important discovery at his laboratory was made accidentally. Rogers' research team was working with a virus called Shope papilloma virus. The name of this tiny organism comes from the doctor who discovered it (Shope) and from the fact that it causes a tumor called a papilloma to form in rabbits that it infects. It is a very good virus to work with because it does not cause any great harm to humans, even if it infects them.

In studying the effects of Shope papilloma virus, the Oak Ridge team discovered that it not only produces tumors, but also causes the rabbits' bodies to make unusually large amounts of an enzyme called *arginase*. This enzyme breaks down the amino acid arginine, and so rabbits infected with the virus have very little arginine in their blood—most of it has been destroyed by the enzyme.

The laboratory workers of the group had regular routine blood tests, to make sure that they were in good health. These tests revealed that the researchers who had worked with the Shope virus had very low amounts of arginine in their blood. Apparently they had caught the virus, and now their bodies were making a great deal of arginase. The virus had introduced its own arginase-making gene into their cells. This effect did not do the scientists any harm, because their bodies could make enough arginine for their needs.

This accidental discovery gave Stanfield Rogers an

idea. If he could find a disease caused by the body's making too much arginine, then he already had a cure for it! It seemed very likely that there might be such a disease, even though no one had reported it yet. For scientists were discovering that all sorts of hereditary errors in the body chemistry could result in children's bodies and minds not developing properly. It had been found, for example, that a failure of the body to use the amino acid phenylalanine properly would result in mental retardation. This disease, called phenylketonuria, can be treated if it is caught early enough, and the child will grow up normally.

In 1969, a pediatrician reported that he had found a family whose children seemed to be suffering from just the disease Rogers was looking for. Two of the children were mentally retarded girls, and tests showed that their bodies did not make any arginase at all. Early in 1970, scientists injected Shope papilloma virus into the girls to see if it would bring the amounts of arginine in their blood down to normal values. Even if the treatment worked, it would be too late to help these children very much. But it would show how other children could be helped by genetic engineering in the future.

In another effort to use genetic engineering to correct mistakes in the code of life, scientists are now trying out a cure for a rare disease called xeroderma pigmentosum. People with this disease have skin that is very sensitive to sunlight—so sensitive that they usually get skin cancer and die by the age of 20. Studies of DNA provided the key to the cause of this disease and suggested a possible cure.

When ultraviolet rays, such as those found in sunlight, strike DNA, they can cause breaks or other damages in the DNA strands. These damages may eventually lead to mutations. But the cells have a special repair system, which helps them to locate the damaged portions of DNA and repair them. According to Arthur Kornberg, who has been studying this repair system, it consists of three main enzymes. One of them is called *endonuclease*. Its job is to patrol the DNA strands and find and mark any damaged portions. The second enzyme, DNA polymerase (the same enzyme that Kornberg used in synthesizing a phage chromosome), finds the marks, cuts out the damaged portions, and strings together the proper series of bases to replace it. Then the third enzyme, DNA-joining enzyme (the one that Khorana used to synthesize a gene), links the "replacement part" into the main strand.

Patients with xeroderma pigmentosum seem to be missing one of these key repair enzymes: endonuclease. There is a virus, called *SV-40*, which may be able to supply the missing gene. Now scientists are testing this virus on human cells from xeroderma pigmentosum patients to see whether it will really work. If it does, and if the virus is found to be safe for humans, this genetic disease will be cured.

Sending a virus "repairman" into the body to supply a missing gene is one way to cure a genetic disease. But this is not the only possible way. Some of the body cells, missing a key enzyme or other chemical, could be taken out, "fixed" by inserting the appropriate gene into their DNA, and then put back into the body. Geneticists already have some experimental evidence that this kind of treatment may work. They have mixed cells of different species of animals—mice and chicks, for example—together in a test tube and treated them with certain chemicals. Tests showed that at least one of the chick genes was actually attached to the DNA of the mouse cells. But if this kind of technique is ever to be used to treat genetic diseases, another problem must be overcome. Usually if cells from a different species, or even a different individual are injected into an animal, its body attacks the "foreigners" violently and destroys them. Scientists thought that combination cells, with genes from two different species, would have the identifying chemicals from both species. If this were so, and the chick-mouse cells were injected back into the sick mouse, its body would react against them and destroy the genes that could have cured it. But instead it was found that the combination cells do not have any identifying chick chemicals on their surface. And so the mouse's body should accept them without any trouble. The next step will be to check this by actually treating mice with a genetic disease, using their own cells with chick genes added. If the mice are cured, and their bodies do not react against the chick chemicals, this will be a very hopeful finding. It will mean that if doctors could add the needed genes to cells from a person with a genetic disease, they would not have to worry about where the genes came from. They might be able to use genes from other animals, without causing the patient's body to fight against the repaired cells.

As scientists unravel the secrets of the code of life, they are opening up many other new frontiers of ge-

A lizard *(Anolis)* with regenerating tail.

netics research, which may some day have a great effect on our lives.

For example, we know that each set of chromosomes contains the plans for the whole body, but only a small fraction of these genes are "turned on" in any particular cell at any particular time. In an eye cell, only the genes for its own functions are working; the ear genes and heart genes and toe genes and the genes for all the other parts of the body are not doing anything. Yet sometimes, genes that have been turned off can be turned back on. When you cut yourself, some of your cells begin to multiply rapidly and move in to fill up the wound and replace the damaged tissues. Plants and some animals can even replace missing parts. Many lizards can grow a new tail to replace one that has broken off. Under certain conditions, a salamander can grow a new leg, and a flatworm can even replace a missing head, brain and all! These new parts are formed by the multiplication of cells whose genes for blood vessels, nerves, and so on were all turned off before the accident. Indeed, even the genes that caused these cells to multiply were turned off before the animal lost its original body part.

If scientists can learn how to turn genes on and off, they will be able to cure many diseases and repair bodies badly damaged by accidents. They will be able to turn off the genes that cause cancer cells to multiply wildly. If a heart or lung is damaged, they will be able to grow a replacement organ by turning on the right genes. Such an organ may be grown right in the body, or it may be grown in the laboratory and then put in by an operation. Perhaps scientists will even be able to change the genes, and make the new organ better than the old one was.

Some researchers think that it will some day be possible to grow identical twins of people from cells in the laboratory. They are already well on the way to this. Carrots and trees have been grown from a few cells. And scientists have raised full-grown frogs using the blueprints provided by the genes from skin or intestinal cells. Most of the genes in these cells are normally turned off. If the cells were placed in a culture dish and given the proper salts and moisture and nutrients, all they would grow into would be new skin or intestinal cells. Sometimes they might change into cancer-like cells. But something very different happens if the nucleus from a skin or intestinal cell is taken out of the cell and placed inside a frog egg cell. (The egg cell's own nucleus is first taken out and thrown away.) Amazingly, the proper genes are now turned

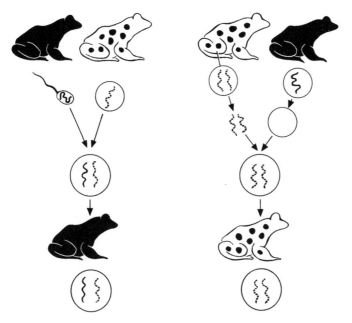

Normal reproduction to the left, with offspring receiving half its genes from each of two parents. Cloning reproduction to the right, with all genes received from one parent only.

on and off in just the right sequence, and a normal frog develops. Its "parent" was the frog from which the nucleus was taken, and it has exactly the same set of chromosomes—it is the identical twin of its parent!

This odd form of reproduction, called *cloning*, may some day be used to breed large numbers of agricultural animals. For example, a few scrapings from the skin of a champion egg-laying hen could provide the blueprints for raising hundreds of her identical twins. Scientists have not yet used the technique for mammals, because their egg cells are much smaller and more difficult to work with. But they think that some day it may be possible to "clone" human beings, too.

Some people—even some scientists—feel frightened about the new power that man is gaining to change his own heredity. They fear that man will not know how to use this power wisely, and may create monsters or try to change people against their wills. Some have even suggested that research in genetics be slowed down. But many geneticists argue that we must try to help the people who suffer from hereditary diseases. Each year a quarter of a million American children are born with birth defects. And there are millions of people whose intelligence is lower than normal. Many of these may some day be helped through genetic engineering. Never before have scientists had so much hope of learning to use the secrets of the code of life to bring good health and sound bodies to the people of this world.

Index

Index